TABLE OF CONTENTS

DISCLAIMER AS WELL AS LAWFUL TAKES NOTE..0

MATERIAL CONNECTION DISCLOSURE: 1

INTRODUCTION 1

¿HOW DOES AFFILIATE MARKETING WORK? 2

UNDERSTANDING YOUR CHOSEN PROGRAM 3

    Clickbank® 4

    Payspree 12

    Paydotcom 13

    Rapbank 14

    E-addict 16

    Click2sell 17

OTHER AFFILIATE METHODS NETWORK 19

STYLE AFFILIATE PROGRAMS 19

DIFFERENT COMMISSION STRUCTURES 21

PROMOTING YOUR CHOSEN PRODUCT 23

DO'S AND DON'TS 25

DISCLAIMER AS WELL AS LAWFUL TAKES NOTE.

The data introduced in this eBook speaks to the perspectives on the distributer as of the date of distribution. The distributer holds the rights to adjust and refresh their feelings dependent on new conditions. This eBook is for educational purposes as it were. The creator and the distributer don't acknowledge any obligations regarding any liabilities coming about because of the utilization of this data. While each endeavor has been made to check the data gave here, the creator and the distributer can't accept any accountability for mistakes, errors or oversights.

Any likenesses with individuals or realities are accidental. No piece of this eBook might be replicated or communicated in any structure, electronic, or mechanical, including copying, recording, or by any instructive stockpiling or recovery framework without communicated composed, dated and marked consent from the distributer.

In accordance with the Federal Trade Commission Guidelines:

MATERIAL CONNECTION DISCLOSURE:

The distributer of this book might be or has a partner relationship and additionally another material association with the suppliers of merchandise and enterprises referenced in this book and might be remunerated when you buy from any of the connections contained thus.

You ought to consistently perform due constancy prior to purchasing merchandise or administrations from anybody by means of the Internet or disconnected.

INTRODUCTION

Associate Marketing is plain and essentially a strategy for advertising where you can procure a commission or expense for advancing different people groups items or administrations.

You, the Affiliate consent to advance those items and additionally benefits by means of your site page, your blog, your email crusades or whatever technique is permitted, and any business you cause will to procure you the Affiliate a set expense/commission or a concurred rate installment.

Subsidiary Marketing whenever done right can be exceptionally worthwhile, numerous individuals make a decent living just by advancing different people groups items.

As an Affiliate Marketer, you don't need to stress over making your own item and you won't need to manage clients or client care issues.

Your fundamental range of abilities expected to turn into an Affiliate Marketer is some essential web promoting information and all the more significantly "the craving to succeed"

There are bunches of various approaches to get fruitful at Affiliate Marketing and there are loads of various projects, shippers and merchants out there who are more than ready to pay you their Affiliate a nice level of commission over to you for advancing their items.

With most member programs the normal commission you can acquire is among 30% and at times 100% in spite of the fact that found the middle value of out, half is a more reasonable benchmark. There are loads of partner programs out there, and most of them are totally for nothing out of pocket to join.

Offshoot Marketing can, when done right, be extremely beneficial.

¿HOW DOES AFFILIATE MARKETING WORK?

At the point when you join a partner promoting program, you are either given a special distinguishing number or name or you pick your own novel identifier. No two individuals in a similar program have a similar number or name. Your connection is explicit to you and only you.

The program administrator at that point utilizes this exceptional identifier to follow all the leads/guests you ship off their site. At the point when one of these leads/guests buys "You" are credited with the deal and allotted the rate commission for that deal. 95% of member programs have dependable global positioning frameworks set up.

At the point when you send a guest to the program proprietors' site, that guest is "logged" as having been shipped off the site by means of your special member interface, regardless of whether they don't buy on the main visit, quite possibly when they return sometime in the future to buy, you can in any case get credited for the deal, this is on the grounds that most projects use "treats" to store data about their guests, as long the guest you initially sent hasn't got another treat or erased/cleared their treats on their PC you are as yet credited with the deal for that guest.

In the event that you've ever pondered, that is the motivation behind why these huge name advertisers consistently reveal to you how to erase your treats before you go to arrange something that they are advancing. They do this for two reasons. One they need to guarantee that they get credited for the deal and two, that you get their rewards they are advertising.

All projects work contrastingly and it's a smart thought to attempt to discover what framework your program proprietor is utilizing. For instance, with Clickbank® it is consistently the last treat that gets the deal apportioned to their record. With others, it tends to be the primary treat or a treat that is for a set timeframe.

UNDERSTANDING YOUR CHOSEN PROGRAM

All merchants will have rules that you should cling to, ensure you peruse and get them. It is no utilization sometime later saying you didn't know about their terms and conditions, most associate projects have a container that you tick to state you have perused perceived and so on, all merchants will won't pay and won't pay partners who don't stick to their terms.

What are the program seller's terms and conditions for installment? Is there a base sum you need to acquire in commission before they will pay you out?

Is this sum feasible?

Is there a base model you need to meet to get paid? For instance, Clickbank® has an exacting Customer Distribution Requirement that you should meet before you get your first payout.

Is there a requirement for you to have your own PayPal account? Any merchant utilizing the Rapid Action Profits contents won't have the option to pay you your 100% bonus in the event that you don't have a Premier or Business account confirmed at PayPal.

By what means will your merchant pay you? Do you need a financial balance? Do you need a PayPal Account? Will they direct charge installment to you? What amount would they say they will charge you to get your bonus? Indeed, believe it or not! They charge YOU to get Your Money.

We will examine different projects in more profundity on the following not many pages. There isn't one that is awesome, however there are some that truly are superior to other people.

Clickbank®

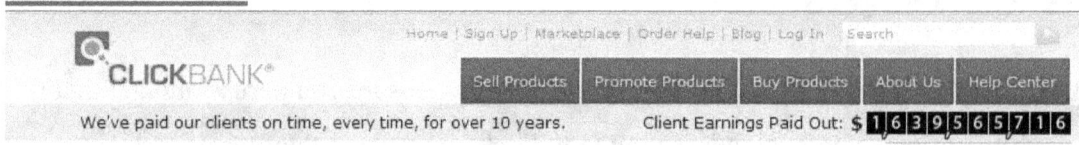

Clickbank® has been around as a computerized commercial center for more than 10 years, it is a grounded program with an abundance of items in its commercial center for you to browse. It cost nothing to join to Clickbank® and make a record as an member.

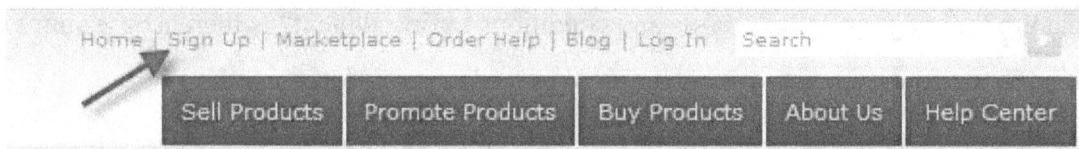

On the top menu bar click the connection that says Sign Up. Fill in all the subtleties also, consent to their terms and conditions.

One piece of their structure requests that you select a record moniker this must be a mix of 5-10 letters and digits.

Select an account nickname for your new account
Account Nickname ǂ (5-10 letters & digits):*

Pick something that you will handily recall, this epithet is the way to signing into your Clickbank® account.

When you have your record fully operational, you would then be able to go to their commercial center and look at all the items they have accessible for you to advance.

Clickbank® Offers solid following and their valuable detailing segment permits you to see bunches of data about your record.

Weekly Sales Snapshot

Week Ending	Gross Sales
2010-09-15 (current week)	$0.00
2010-09-08	$3.93
2010-09-01	$0.00
2010-08-25	$0.00
2010-08-18	$0.00

Daily Sales Snapshot

Mon	Sep	13	$0.00
Sun	Sep	12	$0.00
Sat	Sep	11	$0.00
Fri	Sep	10	$0.00
Thu	Sep	09	$0.00
Wed	Sep	08	$0.00
Tue	Sep	07	$0.00
Mon	Sep	06	**$0.00**
Sun	Sep	05	$3.93
Sat	Sep	04	$0.00
Fri	Sep	03	$0.00
Thu	Sep	02	$0.00
Wed	Sep	01	$0.00
Tue	Aug	31	$0.00
Mon	Aug	30	**$0.00**

You can bore down as much as you'd like. With this record, you can see there has been recently the one deal in the entire fourteen day time frame.

This was on Sunday 05th September – we can penetrate down and get to the deal to discover more data about it. In the week after week deals report, click on the week the deal was made. 2010-09-08 another window opens up and will show the subtleties of all exchanges made in that week.

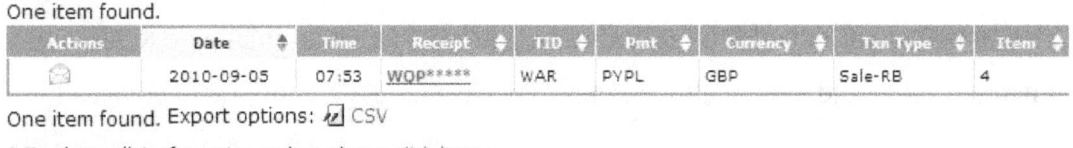

Here you can see the date and time the exchange occurred. The receipt number is asterisked in light of the fact that this is a subsidiary deal. The TID is one that I set to follow this specific item. (More on that later) The Pmt shows me that the buyer paid through their PayPal account, they paid in GBP and it is a repetitive regularly scheduled installment (Sale-RB)

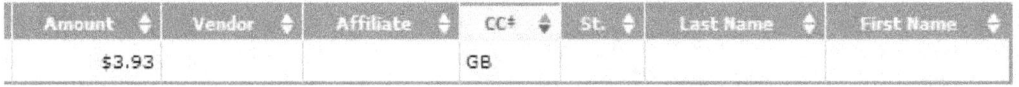

The following part of the screen shows the measure of commission procured, it would likewise give you the epithet of the seller and the member related with the deal which nation the client came from and what their genuine last name and first name were, (I've altered those subtleties out for security reasons) Clickbank® has a magnificent quest dashboard for you to utilize.

Clickbank® has in a real sense a huge number of items for you to advance a new expansion is the capacity to "Social Promote" so you can even procure commissions on prescribing items to your Facebook companions. To utilize this component ensure you sign into your ClickBank account, before you make your hoplink.

Making Your Hoplinks to advance Products

Whenever you have chosen your items you need to elevate then you need to make your hoplink – recall this is your extraordinary identifier to the framework.

Suppose my Niche is the Pet specialty, so I have gone to the commercial center, chosen the class "Home and Garden" a sub classification of this segment is designated "Creature Care and Pets" that is the segment I need to take a gander at.

Clickbank illuminates me there are 381 items recorded and to look over in this segment of their commercial center. We need to bore down considerably further to discover our item to advance.

Here we can sort the items as indicated by our necessities.

We are searching for an item that is famous, has a sensible payout sum and has a high gravity score. The gravity score reveals to us that different associates are effectively advancing this item as well.

In a perfect world, we are searching for an item that as of now has some associate devices we can use to advance it, lamentably not a ton of them do.

The item above meets the standards we are searching for. The payout is just shy of $20, and it has a sensible gravity score of 59.44 there are additionally some acceptable offshoot instruments given to you to advance it. The connection to the offshoot page isn't right, however you can get to the instruments from their site without any problem.

Their offshoot apparatuses page is situated here

http://www.buildingachickencoop.com/affiliates.html

We will advance this item, we click the advance catch and another screen opens us like this one. In the event that you are signed into your Clickbank account, your epithet will effectively be appearing in the top box. The subsequent box is for any following ID you need to add.

Adding a following ID is helpful to help you to remember where you are advancing the item and which real item it is. For this model we will pick a following ID that distinguishes the item so we input "plans" as the following ID. Next hit the make button and your new scrambled connection is made for you with the TID.

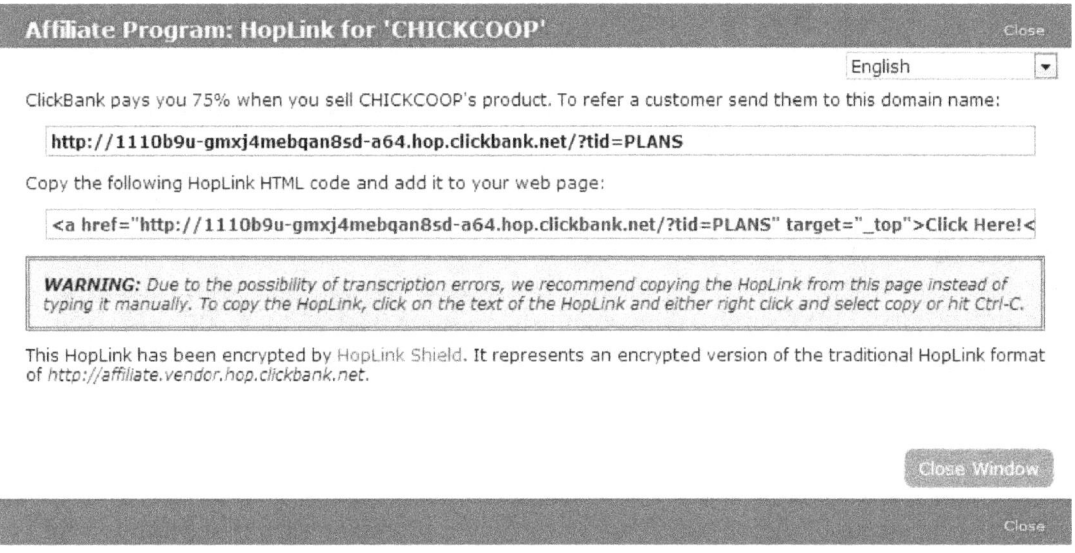

Reorder the connections to a book record on your PC try to save the document for future reference. I have all my partner joins saved in a record on the work area and it's basically called "Offshoot Links"

Presently we have our interesting ID we will utilize this to advance the item. We should perceive how to weave it together.

From the partner page, proceed to choose a picture to utilize and add it to your site page or blog. The flag one is quite spotless and the correct size.

Leaderboard 728 X 90 - Image Above Shrunk To Fit

We need to save this picture to our PC, so right snap on it and pick "save as".

The following stage is to transfer the picture to our facilitating space/site.

Spot the image into your pictures organizer inside your public_html envelope. We have named the picture chickens3.jpg.

To add the picture total with the associate connection, we have added the accompanying content to a book gadget in our wordpress topic. The subject we are utilizing considers one pioneer board style add to be added to the highest point of the relative multitude of pages/posts. By adding the code there, our advert and associate connection will be appeared on all the locales pages.

Here is the code the primary line <a href="http://1110b9u-gmxj4mebqan8sda64.hop.clickbank.net/?tid=PLANS" target="_top"> is our associate connection and the second line <img src="http://chickenrearing.com/pictures/chickens3.jpg"> advises the page where to search for the picture to show to the guest.

<a href="http://1110b9u-gmxj4mebqan8sd-a64.hop.clickbank.net/?tid=PLANS" target="_top">

<img src="http://chickenrearing.com/pictures/chickens3.jpg"></a>

At the point when anybody taps on that picture they are taken to the business page for the item and bring with it our member ID, so we can get credited for the deal. The lower part of the ClickBank request structure will show [affiliate= your clickbank ID. Your Tracking ID.

Copyright © 2010 Click Sales Inc. ClickBank / 917 Lusk St / Suite 200 / Boise ID 83706.  Secure Payments

[affiliate = js33ukms.plans]

At the point when anybody arranges the item having come from our site, we get credited with the deal and acquire the 75% commission guaranteed.

In the event that there is a discount mentioned, their framework naturally deals with that and deducts any granted commissions from your record.

All snaps are recorded and followed by Clickbank and all installments to the merchant and the member are prepared by Clickbank. You needn't bother with a PayPal record to be a Clickbank offshoot anyway you do require an ordinary financial records. You need to meet their severe Customer Distribution Requirement before they will pay out your first bonus check.

Payspree

http://payspree.com Free to join to as an offshoot, their items remunerations rates range from half to 100% commissions.

Payspree charges a little expense from each deal. The expense is payable by either the merchant or the partner dependant upon who the deal was credited to. Expenses are paid to the program administrator consistently toward the beginning of every month. Payspree as of now has 274 items recorded in its commercial center.

Payspree doesn't work a similar route as Clickbank by sharing every individual deal it works by dividing the deals among the seller and the member. Except if you are advancing a 100% commission item, the main deal you make, consistently goes to the item merchant.

Here's how sales will be paid out at each level.

Sale #	50%	60%	75%	100%
1	Vendor	Vendor	Vendor	Affiliate
2	Affiliate	Affiliate	Affiliate	Affiliate
3	Vendor	Affiliate	Affiliate	Affiliate
4	Affiliate	Vendor	Affiliate	Affiliate
5	∞	Affiliate	∞	∞
6		Affiliate		

Partners are answerable for discounting any deals that are credited to their record and hence mentioned to be discounted. On the off chance that you don't discount a deal when a discount is mentioned your record can be crippled. Payspree gives following and revealing measurements like Clickbank.

All installments to both the seller and the associate are assigned through the Payspree framework consequently. You must have a PayPal account to utilize Payspree.

An ordinary associate connection for a Payspree item will resemble this
http://payspree.com/786/Username

Paysprees items are developing and it very well may be beneficial investigating their commercial center to check whether there is an item or two that you could add to your site and advance as a partner.

Paydotcom

http://Paydotcom.com is another commercial center style of framework and has countless classes and items for you to browse.

To join as an offshoot is free, sellers are permitted to pay your payments either with a money order or by PayPal, the larger part pay utilizing PayPal, some will pay through compensation individuals on the web, which tragically eats considerably further into your member payout.

All sellers are answerable for paying their own offshoots by means of whichever strategy they pick.

Paydotcom as of now has a large number of items recorded in its commercial center. You can peruse for items to advance utilizing their online inquiry framework; this framework is fundamentally the same as the one at Clickbank you can look by classifications, subcategories or just by a solitary catchphrase.

Dissimilar to Clickbank where your partner deals are gathered into the one offshoot account and every merchants deals add to the one record, with Paydotcom, as Payspree, every deal you make is dealt with separately and your bonuses are paid exclusively, Payspree does anyway pay these commissions straightforwardly into your PayPal account.

Paydotcom gives following and deals measurements as Raw Clicks, Unique snaps, deals, discounts and change rates.

Affiliate sales:

View All My Affiliate Sales In Last 30 Days

Product Name:	Today:	Yesterday:	Last 7 days:	Last 30 days:
Totals: for all products below	Aff Sales: $0 See details...	Aff Sales: $0 See details...	Aff Sales: $0 See details...	Aff Sales: $12 See details...
Unit price: $27.00	Aff Sales: $0 See details...	Aff Sales: $0 See details...	Aff Sales: $0 See details...	Aff Sales: $12.00 See details...

Some Paydotcom merchants will give you subsidiary instruments to utilize, for example, Standards, instant messages, blog entries, and so on.

To advance any item from Paydotcom, you make your connection from inside your record for the item you need to advance.

An average member connect for a Paydotcom item will resemble this.

http://paydotcom.net/r/87756/AccountName/26107650/

Any seller utilizing the Paydotcom situation has an option to decline to acknowledge you as their member.

Rapbank

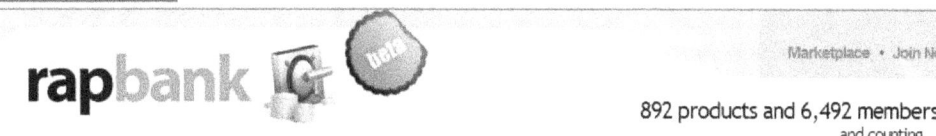

To join to Rapbank as an offshoot again it's Free basically hit the Join presently connect and make your record.

Rapbank is another commercial center where merchants list their advanced items for you to advance. Rapbank is somewhat convoluted and doesn't exactly work equivalent to Clickbank, Payspree or Paydotcom, it's some place in the middle of each of the three. The free record set up is adequate for any individual who is simply taking a gander at turning into an associate for any item recorded at Rapbank.

Insights for your record will show you the number of deals you have made, the number of snaps have been made and how much commission you have produced using advancing every item.

This is what a normal member interface resembles for a Rapbank item.
http://rapbank.com/go/1846/112/make-money-blogging.html

You can advance entire classifications from the Rapbank Marketplace http://112.rapbank.com/products/category/affiliate-marketing/ or simply the entire commercial center itself by utilizing http://112.rapbank.com/items/as you can likely tell from these connections, our record ID at Rapbank is 112

Rapbank was made as a spot where all Rapid Action Profits content proprietors could get together and list their things available to be purchased. The advantage to the partners is that you have a spot to go to locate these moment paying commission items this is much simpler than looking through Google for destinations "fueled by Rapid Action Profits".

At the point when you advance an item through Rapbank, Rapbank doesn't pay you, the merchant of the item pays you naturally using their content, since all Rap Bank recorded item proprietors utilize similar content as their business, member and promoting framework, the commissions are paid a similar way the Payspree framework works.

On the off chance that you have been paid for a deal and, at that point hence the buyer demands a discount, you as the Affiliate should respect that discount. All Rapid Action Profits content clients reserve a privilege to decline to have you as their Affiliate and can restrict your record from inside their dashboard.

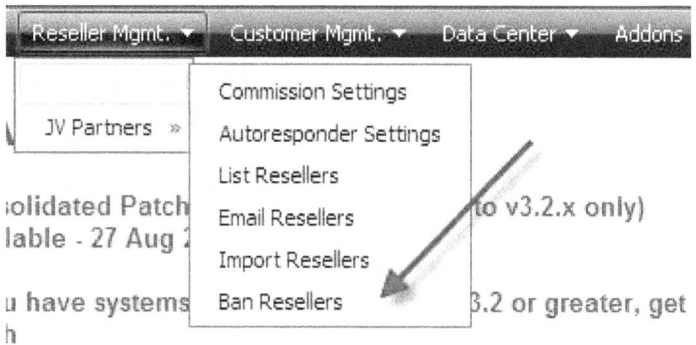

E-addict

E-addict sells both computerized and unmistakable merchandise and presently reports to have 8500 dynamic dealers. E-addict doesn't have a commercial center isolated into classes or subcategories, and it tends to be truly hard to track down your specialty related items to advance.

With E-addict every dealer is answerable for their own associate plan and characterize their own terms and conditions, for example what commission rate they will pay, how frequently they will pay you, what cash they will pay you in and the degree of commissions you need to meet before installment is made to you.

As a subsidiary advancing a sellers item at e-addict you do gain admittance to the essential measurements of the number of deals you have made for that specific merchant, there is no announcing of navigates your associate connections.

Click2sell

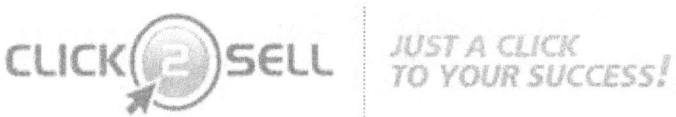

Click2sell presently records more than 871 items in their commercial center; you can look through the commercial center by class or sub classification, you can see the prominence, or % of deals made by partners and so on

Pursuing a member account is free, click2sell pay commissions three weeks after the month end and you can choose to be paid either through PayPal or MoneyBookers and in a decision of cash.

Click2sell give sensible initially measurements for you to look through. As this is a recently opened record, there isn't anything to see, yet the image on the following page will give you a thought of their announcing capacity.

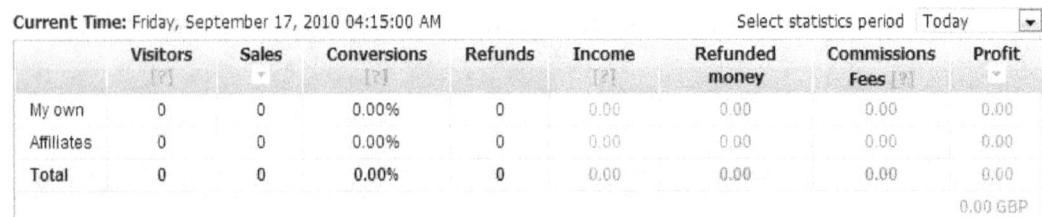

At the point when you are taking a gander at which items to advance through their commercial center you can tap on more data and get definite data with respect to both the merchant and the item.

Product Details

Merchant Name:	Ebiz Depot (contact)
Merchant Pays Via:	PayPal
Merchant Rank:	0.0%
Product Price:	29.99 USD
Earn %:	50.00%
Earn USD:	15.00 USD
Date Added:	22-04-2009

You additionally will see point by point item data how it changes over, what the discount rate resembles how famous it is and where the deals are made. As should be obvious from this screen shot, this item is chiefly sold through subsidiaries; and the discount rate is 8%.

Product Statistics

[?]	Conversion %:	0.62%
[?]	Refund %:	8.00%
[?]	Affiliate Sales %:	91.00%
[?]	Popularity:	2.18%

Create affiliate link

With click2sell, you have the alternative to make your partner connect that will go directly to the sellers' business page, or you can make your own limited time page for the merchants' item and make your subsidiary connection so it goes straightforwardly to the items checkout page.

The entire click2sell framework is fundamentally the same as Clickbank, with one special case; the sellers need to pay the partners through the framework, as a subsidiary you are not paid by click2sell straightforwardly. Click2sell do express that they restrict sellers from utilizing their framework on the off chance that they don't pay the offshoots their legitimate bonus.

As should be obvious there are a ton of advanced commercial centers to pick your items to advance from, and they are altogether unique in the manner in which they work their frameworks, techniques, detailing, following and installments, you may even locate a similar item recorded at various commercial centers with various commissions being advertised. Take as much time as necessary to glance around and locate the best arrangements before you start your advancements.

A ton of web advertisers like to run their own in house programs as well. On the off chance that you discover an item that you truly like and need to advance it, examine the lower part of the fundamental deals page search for the words "Members" or "Partners" here and there even "Accomplices"

In the event that when you visit the page the offshoot program isn't noticeable use Google to check whether they do have a program you could join.

These two sites contain a rundown of a tremendous number of subsidiary projects that are accessible to join.

http://www.associateprograms.com/and   and   http://www.top-affiliate.com/

OTHER AFFILIATE METHODS NETWORK STYLE AFFILIATE PROGRAMS

There are a few member program networks on the Internet where you can locate a wide scope of shippers in various classes. Recall that despite the fact that these projects are generally on a similar site, they are autonomously possessed and worked by every shipper; the organization just unites the traders in a single spot for the subsidiary to discover.

The subsidiary joins to the organization, the dealer joins to the organization and the organization oversees both the offshoots and the shippers. Instances of organizations are:

Commission Junction: http://www.cj.com.

Commission Junction is one of the main subsidiary program networks with more than 2,000 dealer projects to browse.

Maxbounty http://www.maxbounty.com

ShareaSale http://www.shareasale.com

In the event that you choose to go along with one of the organizations, consistently try to peruse their terms and conditions. Follow their standards and all should be fine. Likewise with different sorts of partner programs, your bonus isn't paid by the organization, however by the individual traders/publicists joined to the organization. For instance MaxBounty express this in their terms and conditions. "Commissions may be procured on Actions revealed by the publicist, and simply after MaxBounty gets full installment from the Advertiser. MaxBounty is under no commitment to pay Affiliates for Actions which are not paid by the Advertiser"

CPA means "Cost Per Action", and contrasted with standard associate advertising, when you advance CPA offers, you can really bring in cash without creating a solitary deal.

This is the most engaging piece of CPA since it gives even the freshest of advertisers the occasion to create a pay. At the point when you send the guest to the customers page and they complete the necessary activity, you get paid for the guest having done whatever was expected of them, be it essentially presenting their email address or phone number into a structure, or rounding out a straightforward short review on the web. In the event that you were liable for sending the guest, you get remunerated for it.

CPA networks work as a "go between" interfacing distributers and sponsors together, they co-ordinate the situation of offers from these distributers and promoters with you the member advertiser. The CPA network takes a charge; or level of the offered cost and pass the rest of the expense onto you the associate advertiser.

Whenever you have been acknowledged into their organization you are given a novel associate connect to advance the proposal from.

Except if you have a high volume of traffic to your site, or are eager to pay to send traffic to your site, it might take you a long effort to get paid by a CPA organization. The base payout limit on most CPA networks is by and large $50.00, so in the event that you are getting $0.50 per email address submitted and just have 5 guests every week, it could take you a drawn-out period of time to hit that base payout edge.

There are different organizations that will pay per perspective on their flag advertisements and so on; again you need a high traffic site to bring in cash from these techniques.

DIFFERENT COMMISSION STRUCTURES

Pay Per Sale: One of the most well-known types of member promoting motivation is called Pay Per Sale (PPS). This is the place where the guest clicks a connection and makes a buy. Your prize is a rate commission for that deal.

You can get the most cash-flow from this kind of offshoot advertising program on things that are considered "high ticket" things, i.e., modern programming like Adobe

(Macromedia) Dreamweaver that retails for $899, a 10% commission of this deal is $89, a 25% commission of this deal is $224.75.

It is significant it is to focus on the measure of the commission rate being advertised. On the off chance that they were just contribution a 2% commission on this equivalent $899 thing you would just acquire $17.98.

On the off chance that there is an assurance period offered with the item sold, you will free your bonus by and large if the buyer restores the item and solicitations a discount.

Pay Per Lead: (PPL) These sort of projects are very famous. With this kind of program, you are paid for each enquiry that comes from your site to the publicist's site, given the guest meets the standards needed by the sponsor. For instance, the guest may must be inside a particular age gathering or have a specific pay level.

Since no buy is included, the odds are higher that the guest will be "changed over" from being a site guest to a planned client when they complete the necessary activity of entering their contact data on the lead structure on the promoter's site.

Commissions for these sort of projects are not as liberal as pay per deal subsidiary projects.

Pay Per Action: (PPA) In this kind of associate promoting program, the promoter pays you when your alluded guest chooses to download a preliminary adaptation of their product or report.

Organizations that offer electronic products and enterprises, for example, distributers, PC and programming organizations rule this specific market. Here and there, lobbies for pay per activity are frequently utilized in mix with pay per deal. The "attempt before you purchase" choice tempts the guest to download the item for a set time for testing.

You are not ensured with this technique for advancement that the guest will at last buy the item, as having attempted it, they probably won't care for it, or they may simply be substance with utilizing the preliminary variant without moving up to the Pro form.

Pay Per Click: (PPC) This technique is regularly utilized by "logical Ad" organizations, Konteratm being the most broadly known one. At the point when a guest drifts over a word their advert put away flies with a connection to a significant item. This is one of the least demanding partner advertising projects to advance, as the substance is as of now there on your site or blog.

Commissions for this sort of program can be little, some as meager as $0.02c per click, payouts can set aside a long effort to accomplish when utilizing this sort of publicizing/subsidiary strategy for advancement.

The busier your site, the more possibility you have of bringing in cash with this sort of partner advancement.

A large portion of the techniques referenced above expect you to have a completely working and as of now filed site or blog.

PROMOTING YOUR CHOSEN PRODUCT

It is significant that you have your own space name and facilitated webpage, regardless of whether this is a blog or a html website doesn't generally make a difference, you won't be viewed as a suitable offshoot to any arrange on the off chance that you don't have and claim your own web presence.

Try not to be enticed to compromise and utilize a free blogger record or free facilitated space, the vast majority of these organizations, don't permit any sort of associate advancement to be run from these sorts of destinations.

On the off chance that you are not kidding about bringing in cash as an associate advertiser you truly need to contribute the couple of dollars needed to have your own space name and facilitating account. It doesn't make a difference if your source this from the least expensive space enlistment center and the least expensive facilitating supplier, however you should be in charge of your own site. Envision the heart split of getting up one morning and finding that your free host has erased all your diligent effort, just don't leave yourself alone helpless before others.

With the plenty of formats accessible to work with, facilitating your own wordpress blog is the fastest and most straightforward approach to set up a web presence. On the off chance that you have no clue about how to set a blog up, there are loads of individuals on

http://www.fiverr.com who will do this for you. Here is a connection to a free download on the most proficient method to set up your blog all alone facilitating account http://www.24hourwordpressguru.com

Attempt and avoid instant formats gave by some associate projects, this is the place where the merchant gives you your own member page. What you truly need is for your site to be special, not a clone of the first. On the off chance that conceivable avoid blazing and pivoting pennants as well.

The items you decide to advance should commend your locales Niche/topic. For instance it is no utilization advancing get rich on the web type items on the webpage http://www.chickenrearing.com anything to be advanced on that website should be identified with, Yes, you got it keeping or raising chickens, or some other type of foul.

We have begun to adapt the site with the Clickbank item and a partner program that will pay 8% commission per deal on any item purchased from the merchants' site. Until further notice that is all we will utilize, we don't need the site to seem as though one major advert, we need the site to be incorporated into a position site, so when the surfer is searching for data on Chickens, they will be coordinated to the site by the web crawlers.

Incorporating your site into a position site requires significant investment and a great deal of devoted difficult work. Attempt to teach yourself to add at any rate one article/post for each day or each other day, use the same number of focused catchphrases in your articles/posts as you can, yet don't be enticed here to utilize too much.

Keep your substance new and state-of-the-art and on subject for your specialty. On the off chance that you have utilized an item you are advancing, compose an inside and out survey on it. State why you like it or don't care for it, show it's sure and negatives and so on by doing this, you are prequalifying for guest and when they leave your site for more data, they'll invest their energy searching for the purchase button, not perusing the business page in extraordinary profundity.

DO'S AND DON'TS

Do's:

- Do ensure you save your subsidiary connects to a book document on your PC.
- Do ensure you save any illustrations to your PC and transfer to your webhosting space.
- Do ensure that your pictures appear on your site.
- Do ensure that the pictures are interactive and go to the correct site when they are tapped on.
- Do watch that your associate connection goes to your member account utilize the following insights gave by the program you are utilizing.

- Do ensure you can acknowledge installments in the money offered by the Vendor/Network.
- Do watch that any CPA offers you are advancing are as yet current; at times crusades are stopped or supplanted by fresher ones.
- Do join subsidiary advertising discussions, pose inquiries, connect and gain from other member advertisers.
- Do ensure that you see any terms and conditions set upon you the subsidiary by the organization you are advancing. Try not to blend programs on the off chance that you are not permitted to.
- Do keep your site current, and in the know regarding new substance.
- Do occasionally test your request connects to guarantee that any merchants' item you are advancing through Clickbank is as yet utilizing Clickbank as their subsidiary program.
- Do intermittently test your connections to items you are advancing and are recorded on PayDotCom, PaySpree or RapBank to guarantee they are still live and in business.
- Do make a solid effort to direct people to your site. In the event that you have time, compose articles on your picked Niche/point and present these to the mainstream article indexes.
- Do participate in conversation discussions identified with your specialty/site subject, utilize the mark record to connect back to your site.

Don'ts:

- Don't anticipate acquiring a fortune short-term, it simply doesn't occur. Any individual who reveals to you in any case is lying.

- Don't disrupt the guidelines of any arrangements you have endorsed with the organizations or other associate program supervisors.
- Don't spam anybody with spontaneous email messages.
- Don't neglect to put a notification on your site and an admonition in your email correspondences so you conform to the FTC rules.
- Don't continue advancing an item or administration in the event that you are not making commissions/deals, or if the seller has made changes to the program.
- Don't neglect to utilize any advertising materials the program seller may have given. Flags, Graphics, email messages or text advertisements. Recall however to avoid any copy content, revise the messages, rephrase the adverts so they are extraordinary to you and your site.
- Don't load your site with bunches of glimmering, pivoting, flickering flags that make it seem as though a firecracker show!
- Don't surrender, in the event that you are dismissed by one organization, attempt another.

www.ingramcontent.com/pod-product-compliance
Lightning Source LLC
Chambersburg PA
CBHW080819220526
45466CB00011BB/3616